Anglo-Saxons
and Vikings

Usborne Quicklinks

The Usborne Quicklinks Website is packed with thousands of links to all the best websites on the internet. The websites include information, video clips, sounds, games and animations that support and enhance the information in Usborne Internet-linked books.

To visit the recommended websites for this book, go to the Usborne Quicklinks Website at **www.usborne-quicklinks.com** and enter the keywords **History of Britain**, then click on the section for Anglo-Saxons and Vikings.

Anglo-Saxons
and Vikings

Hazel Maskell & Dr. Abigail Wheatley

Illustrated by Ian McNee & Giacinto Gaudenzi

Designed by Tom Lalonde

Edited by Ruth Brocklehurst & Jane Chisholm

Consultant: Dr. Ryan Lavelle,
University of Winchester

Contents

6 The invaders strike

8 King Arthur

10 New kingdoms

12 The Anglo-Saxons

18 Death and burials

20 Christianity returns

22 Early monasteries

24 Changes in the north

26 The rise of Mercia

30 Trade and culture

32 Raiders from the sea

34 The Vikings

36 Alfred the Great

40 United kingdoms?

42 Athelstan of England

44 Viking York

46 Edgar the Peaceful

48 Troubled times

52 Chaos and conquest

54 King Canute

56 A messy succession

58 Edward's London

60 End of an era

62 Index

64 Acknowledgements

An age of invasions

In the year 43, the Romans – a powerful empire-building nation from Rome, in Italy – invaded and conquered much of Britain. With them, they brought peace, order, and the Christian religion, and they stayed for over 350 years.

But by the end of the 4th century, Rome's power had begun to decline. The Romans withdrew from Britain in 410, leaving its people fighting among themselves, and vulnerable to invasion once again...

For centuries, the 5th-century invasions have fascinated artists and writers. This is a 13th-century painting of a battle between the Britons and the Saxon invaders.

'...in the streets lay tops of lofty towers, fallen to the ground, stones of high walls, holy altars, fragments of human bodies, covered with blood, looking as if they'd been squeezed together in a press...'

This description of the devastation left by the invaders comes from the account of Gildas, a 6th-century priest.

The invaders strike

From around the year 450, Britain came under attack. Boatloads of warriors from what is now Germany and Denmark launched a series of devastating raids on the south and east coast. The invaders were made up of three main groups – the Angles, the Saxons and the Jutes. These fearsome warriors forced the tribes of native Britons to flee to the hills.

War across the land

A priest named Gildas described how the bloodthirsty invaders fought their way inland. They left ghastly scenes in their wake – bodies lay strewn amidst ransacked or burned buildings. Some of the Britons fought back, but the warriors didn't cease their merciless advance until they had seized most of southern Britain.

Angle-land

Within a few centuries, the land the invaders conquered would be known as England, after the Angles. Its people would call themselves the English.

In the dark

Gildas' version of events probably isn't entirely accurate – it only records one man's point of view. But the invasions took place around 1,500 years ago, and Gildas' is the sole surviving account from around the time.

In fact, there are very few writings from this period at all, and many of the other clues that help historians, such as objects and buildings, haven't survived either. Because historians are more or less in the dark about what was happening at this time, it is sometimes known as the Dark Ages.

It is likely that at least some of the invaders were forced to leave their old homes when their lands were flooded by rising sea levels.

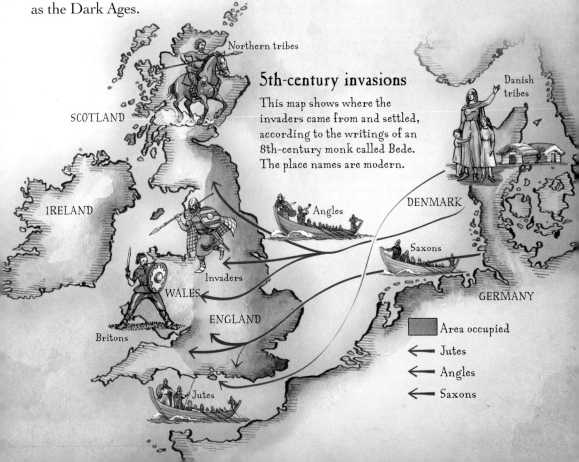

Northern tribes

SCOTLAND

Danish tribes

5th-century invasions

This map shows where the invaders came from and settled, according to the writings of an 8th-century monk called Bede. The place names are modern.

IRELAND

Angles

DENMARK

Saxons

Invaders

WALES

GERMANY

ENGLAND

Britons

Jutes

☐ Area occupied
← Jutes
← Angles
← Saxons

King Arthur

No one knows exactly what happened during the invasion, but it seems the Britons fought hard to resist the invaders. Their struggle became the stuff of legend, woven around the mysterious figure of King Arthur.

Trace memories

Experts are fairly sure that there never was a king of the Britons called Arthur. But some think that stories about him may preserve a faint memory of a leader who united the Britons against the invaders.

Scholars from Wales were the first to mention Arthur in writing. They wanted to show that the Britons had put up a good fight, even though they lost in the end.

Later writers added characters such as Lancelot and Gawain, and tales like the Holy Grail, to create long and complex stories.

Artists and writers have been inspired by the legends of King Arthur for centuries.

This picture was painted in the 14th century. It illustrates a popular story about how, as a young boy, Arthur pulled a magic sword – called Excalibur – from a stone, to prove he was the rightful king. The man beside him in the dark robe is Merlin the magician.

This is how the story of Arthur took shape...

Around 550

Gildas wrote about a general called Ambrosius, who led the Britons to victory against the Angles and Saxons. It's possible the name 'Ambrosius' was mistaken for 'Artorius' or 'Arthur' by later writers.

Around 830

A writer known as Nennius, who was probably from Wales, wrote of a powerful military leader called Arthur who won many battles against the Angles and the Saxons.

Around 1130

A Welsh writer named Geoffrey of Monmouth described how a king named Arthur defeated the Saxons and united the Britons, with the help of Merlin the magician.

1160-90

Chrétien de Troyes, a French writer, wrote many stories about Arthur and his knights, including Lancelot, Gawain and Percival. He described Arthur's court at Camelot and the Quest for the Holy Grail.

1344

King Edward III decided to bring back the noble traditions of King Arthur. He held a tournament called a 'Round Table' at Windsor Castle.

1469-70

Sir Thomas Malory, an English writer, completed his book telling the whole story of Arthur. In 1485, this became one of the first books to be printed in Britain.

1485

Henry Tudor became King of England. His family claimed to be descended from King Arthur, to strengthen their popularity.

1691

Poet John Dryden and composer Henry Purcell wrote the first opera about King Arthur.

1840-1900

Many stories, poems and pictures about King Arthur were created by writers including Alfred Tennyson and Mark Twain and artists such as Gustav Doré and William Morris.

1960

'Camelot' the musical was produced by Alan Jay Lerner and Frederick Loewe. In 1967, it was released as a film, too.

1982

Prince William was born and named William Arthur Philip Louis. His father, Prince Charles, also has 'Arthur' as one of his middle names.

New kingdoms

Despite the Britons' best efforts, by around 600 the south and east of Britain were occupied by the invaders. They brought with them their own types of housing, clothing and ornaments, and their own languages. The native Britons spoke Celtic languages, but the new settlers spoke languages known as 'Germanic', as they came from areas in and around what is now Germany. These people became known as the Anglo-Saxons.

Fortriu

Atholl

Dalriada

Gododdin
Strathclyde
Bernicia
Rheged

Deira

Elmet
Gwynedd   Lindsey

Powys   Mercia
Middle   East
Angles   Angles

Dyfed
Gwent   Hwicce   East Saxons

West   Kent
Saxons   South
Saxons
Dumnonia

Pictish kingdoms
Celtic kingdoms
Anglo-Saxon kingdoms

In around 600, the nations of England, Scotland and Wales didn't exist.
Instead, Britain was divided up into many smaller kingdoms. This map shows some of them.

New rulers

For the Britons in the south and east, being taken over by invaders wasn't anything new – the Romans had settled heavily there too. It's likely that many Britons stayed on in these areas, perhaps working for the Anglo-Saxons and adopting their way of life, their customs and their languages. Over time, several Anglo-Saxon kingdoms – each ruled by a warrior-king – emerged there.

A divided land

Meanwhile, in the west and the north, the Britons kept control. They were probably joined by others fleeing the occupied areas.

In what is now Scotland, a group of Celtic-speakers known as the Scots ruled the small northwestern kingdom of Dalriada. But most of the rest of Scotland was inhabited by people called the Picts, who had managed to resist even the Romans. Very little is known about them – we don't even know what language they spoke.

The Britons in the Celtic kingdoms kept in close contact with each other, through activities such as trading. Although the people in different areas spoke variations of Celtic languages, they still understood one another. They also shared many customs – including their religion, Christianity.

Celtic revival

In the face of the newcomers, the Britons clung to their Celtic heritage and even revived some of their ancient traditions. In the west of England, they rebuilt old forts first built by their ancestors before Roman times. They also adapted the ancient Celtic swirling style of decoration, using it to adorn not only traditional metalwork, but new Christian books. Soon, both the Britons' stylish craftwork and their religion would have a huge impact on Anglo-Saxon culture.

Meanwhile, in the Anglo-Saxon kingdoms, a very different way of life was taking shape...

This bowl was probably made by British metalworkers, in the late 6th or early 7th century – over 1,300 years ago. It is made of beaten metal, with swirling Celtic-style decorations of red, blue and green enamel and glass.

This is Cadbury Hillfort in the southwest of England. It is one of the ancient forts the Celtic Britons rebuilt, possibly to use as a stronghold in their fight against the Saxon invaders.

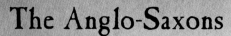

The Anglo-Saxons

Many of the Anglo-Saxons were born fighters. They started fighting as soon as they jumped from their ships, and battled their way inland – taking more land as they needed it. And at the head of each attack, there was an Anglo-Saxon king leading the charge.

Duties and dangers

These are Anglo-Saxon drinking horns, used at feasts. The metal rims and tips are from the 6th century, while the horns are replicas.

The original horns haven't survived, but they would have come from giant cattle called aurochs. These animals are now extinct.

Being an Anglo-Saxon king was hard work. He was expected to lead his warriors into battle, reward them for their loyalty, and make sure his people had enough land to grow crops and keep livestock. There were always new threats to deal with too – either from rival kingdoms, or from scheming followers who wanted to be king themselves. So kings needed to be not only strong fighters, but also good judges of character.

There were no rules about who succeeded a king, so the time just after a king died was particularly dangerous. Many men could step up to claim his place, often with bloody consequences.

Living like a king

Each king was surrounded by a council of advisers, known as a *witan*. This group may have included nobles, priests and members of the king's family.

Despite all the hard work and dangers that a king faced, there were many rewards. He claimed a share of food from every farmer in his territory, which meant that he and his followers never went hungry. And he took the lion's share of treasures won in battle, so a successful king could become very rich. The most powerful ones of all even claimed valuable gifts from lower kings called underkings, or *ealdormen*, who promised support in return for protection or peace.

Ruling classes

When he wasn't on the battlefield, a king lived in a big wooden house, called a hall, with his bravest and most loyal warriors. A king's hall was built to impress his subjects, and to hold important meetings. But it was also a cheerful home, with a blazing fire, rich tapestries hanging on the walls and rushes strewn over the floor.

A king plied his warriors with gifts, such as rings, jewels, land and weapons, to make sure they stayed with him. So being a king was an expensive business. No wonder Anglo-Saxon kings were always raiding each other's territory for more loot and land.

Here an Anglo-Saxon king is holding a feast in his hall. The roof has been cut away so you can see inside.

The guests are eating meat cooked over the fire, and drinking ale, while a poet tells them stories set to music.

Everyday life

Most Anglo-Saxon settlers lived as farmers. Each farmer usually owned enough land to grow food for a family – an area known as a *hide*. The man who owned it was called a *ceorl* (pronounced *churl*).

Ceorls and their families lived near their fields, in houses made from sturdy wooden frames, finished off with mud and reeds. A man who owned more than five hides of land was called a *thegn* (pronounced *thane*). Thegns lived in halls, and were second only to kings.

Many Britons probably farmed alongside the Anglo-Saxons, and were gradually absorbed into their society.

Eating and drinking

The Anglo-Saxons ate simple, hearty food. They made stews and soups, baked bread and brewed beer. Their farm animals provided them with meat, eggs, feathers, wool and milk, which they churned into butter or made into cheese. They also grew many kinds of fruit in their gardens, and kept bees for their honey.

This illustration from a late Anglo-Saxon book shows two farmers with huge tools known as scythes, which they used to harvest their crops.

This reconstructed Anglo-Saxon village shows the kind of houses in which ordinary workers would have lived.

The pecking order

From kings to ceorls, Anglo-Saxon men led very active, often violent, lives. Even farmers had to be ready to fight for their king whenever necessary. All fighters carried long spears with iron points, and some also had sharp iron knives, paid for out of their own pockets. The richest had swords.

Anglo-Saxon women were in charge of spinning and weaving thread, as well as sewing and caring for clothes, bedlinen and furnishings. They also brewed and served drinks such as ale and *mead*, a strong drink made from honey.

At the bottom of the pecking order were slaves. Some slaves were born into slave families; others became slaves through poverty, or after being captured in wars. They had to do all the hardest and dirtiest jobs.

These Anglo-Saxon spearheads would have been used for hunting and fighting. The wooden handles are modern – the original ones rotted away hundreds of years ago.

Crime and punishment

Anglo-Saxon kings laid down the laws of the land, and set out the consequences for breaking them. These 'lawcodes' were especially concerned with violent crimes, from injuries inflicted in brawls, to murders. It must have been a rough world.

The Anglo-Saxons had a strong sense of family loyalty. If any member of their family was murdered, they felt it was fair to kill someone from the murderer's family, unless they received money or goods in compensation. Laws set out how much compensation, or *wergeld*, was owed for different victims – more for thegns, less for ceorls, and less again for women and slaves.

"Ten vats of honey, 300 loaves of bread, 42 measures of ale, two cows or ten sheep, ten geese, 20 hens, ten cheeses, one measure of butter, five salmon, 100 eels..."

List of goods collected from every ten families each year for their king

Anglo-Saxon farmers had to give their king a share of their crops and animals.

Changing language

Unlike the Celtic-speaking Britons, some of whom understood the Romans' language of Latin, and could read and write, the Anglo-Saxons spoke Germanic languages, and weren't very good at reading or writing. When they did write, they used symbols called runes, although later they learned to use the Roman alphabet, like the Britons.

This gold medallion is marked with some of the first Old English runes. Experts think they refer to the wolf that's shown.

Gradually, the Anglo-Saxons' languages merged and spread to become what is now known as Old English. After many shifts, it became the English language that is spoken today. Many words in modern English point back to Anglo-Saxon times, and English place names often have Old English roots, such as *ham* meaning 'farm', *cester* or *chester* meaning 'old Roman city', and *ing* meaning 'people of'.

Dressing up

Early Anglo-Saxons wove cloth from wool and linen, dyed with plant juices. Their clothes were warm and practical, but they sometimes piled on lots of ornaments too.

Clothes and fashion

Anglo-Saxons all wore loose-fitting tunics. Women's tunics came down to their ankles, but men wore knee-length tunics over cloth leggings. These were gathered at the waist with a belt, which was also used to carry knives, keys and other tools.

For extra warmth, people wore cloaks which they fixed in place with brooches. They also had leather shoes and bags, and ornaments such as beads and metal clasps. Everyone dressed alike, and even kings and nobles just wore more luxurious versions of the same clothes and accessories that everyone else wore.

Early Anglo-Saxon women usually went bare-headed. But by the later Anglo-Saxon period, most women covered their hair with a hood known as a wimple.

Pagan beliefs

The Anglo-Saxons were pagans, which means they worshipped many gods. They believed these gods were in charge of different aspects of life. Fittingly for a warrior people, the gods they revered most – such as Woden and Thunor – were gods of the battlefield.

But, as many Anglo-Saxons were farmers rather than fighters, nature was also a key part of their religion. All across the countryside they set up shrines to gods of rocks, trees and other natural things that they held sacred. Many religious festivals were also connected with events in the farming year, such as harvest time.

Telling tales

The Anglo-Saxons loved tales of danger and adventure. But, as they could barely read or write, stories had to be passed along by being recited, memorized and retold – usually as songs, which were easier to learn. They told of heroes, kings, monsters and faraway places, and were usually about bravery, loyalty, good and evil.

As well as providing entertainment, these tales also gave the Anglo-Saxons a way of passing on their history. Long after they had settled in Britain, many of their stories were still about legendary Germanic heroes, and the lands they had left behind.

Week days

The Anglo-Saxons named days of the week after their important gods:

Tiw's day (Tuesday) Tiw was the god of bravery and fighting.

Woden's day (Wednesday) Woden was the chief of the gods.

Thunor's day (Thursday) Thunor was the god of war and thunder.

Frig's day (Friday) Frig was the goddess of love and beauty.

This is an 8th-century Anglo-Saxon box lid, carved with gods and heroes. Above the figure on the right with the bow and arrow are some runes spelling his name – ᚠᚪᛁᛚ – which translates as *Aegil*.

Death and burials

In 1938, a landowner named Edith Pretty asked a local archaeologist, Basil Brown, to investigate some mysterious mounds on her grounds at Sutton Hoo, in Suffolk. Brown discovered the remains of a huge ship, buried over a thousand years before. Halfway along it was a chamber, containing one of the most astounding hoards of Anglo-Saxon riches ever seen.

It was the burial place of a powerful 7th-century king. Although the body had decayed long ago, historians think he may have been Raedwald, King of the East Angles, who died around the year 625.

The ship burial at Sutton Hoo may have looked something like this. The walls of the chamber have been cut away, so you can see inside.

Experts assume that the ship, which was over 27m (88 feet) long, was dragged up a steep slope from the River Deben nearby.

The ship was laid in a trench, and a mound was built over it.

The chamber held weapons, treasures and everyday items.

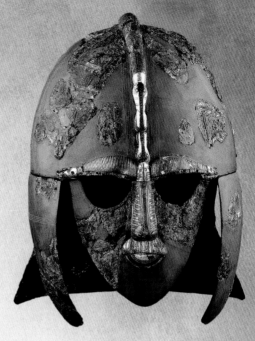

This iron helmet was buried with the king at Sutton Hoo, and may have been used as his crown. Archaeologists found it all in bits, but they've painstakingly pieced it back together.

Merchants and traders

The Sutton Hoo discovery gave historians a rare glimpse into the wealth of an Anglo-Saxon king, and showed how well-connected the Anglo-Saxons were to other countries. Among the treasure, there were coins from France, silver bowls from the Mediterranean, cloth from Syria, and dishes from Byzantium and Egypt.

It made them realize that the early Anglo-Saxon era wasn't just about farming and fighting. It was also a time of trade with distant lands.

Ashes to ashes

Boat burials like that at Sutton Hoo were actually very rare, and were limited to only the richest, most powerful men. Most Anglo-Saxons were cremated. The ashes were put in an urn and then buried in a shared cemetery. These remains were often buried alongside objects such as rings, brooches, beads, weapons and tools, which may have been intended for use in an afterlife.

But, during the 7th century, Anglo-Saxon attitudes to life and death began to undergo a huge change.

Life and death

An Anglo-Saxon fable tells of a sparrow, flying from a dark, stormy night through a bright, busy hall, then back out again.

The short time in the hall represents life, and that spent outside is all that's unknown about what happens before and after.

19

Saint David

Christian Britons in Wales were too busy fighting the Anglo-Saxons to try to convert them.

According to a later legend, a religious leader named Dewidd told the Britons to attach leeks to their hats, so they could see each other clearly on the battlefield.

Dewidd is now known as Saint David and the leek is now a Welsh national emblem.

This map shows some of the main monasteries in 7th century Britain.

Iona
Lindisfarne
Hexham   Jarrow
Ripon   Whitby
Repton
Peterborough   Ely
London
Glastonbury   Canterbury

The Anglo-Saxon invasions dealt a sharp blow to Christianity in Britain. As the pagan warriors drove most of the Christian Britons from their lands, Britain became an island largely ruled by pagans.

But, by the late 6th century, the Anglo-Saxons had settled down into organized, fairly peaceful kingdoms. Church leaders in Ireland and Italy saw their chance to bring back Christianity as the main religion in Britain.

They started by sending monks – men who had dedicated their lives to their faith – as missionaries to try to convert the Anglo-Saxon kings to Christianity. If the kings converted, then the ordinary people would almost certainly follow.

Columba

One of the first successful missionaries was an Irishman named Columba. Around 563, he founded a religious community, or monastery, on the island of Iona. This island had been given to him by the Scots king, who was already a Christian.

From there, Columba founded several churches in the region and set out to convert the pagan Picts. As the Christian message spread, monks from Iona moved south into Anglo-Saxon kingdoms, setting up new monasteries as they went.

Augustine

Meanwhile, monks from Rome in Italy were targeting the south of Britain, on the orders of their leader, Pope Gregory. In 597, he sent a monk named Augustine to meet the most powerful Anglo-Saxon king, Aethelbert of Kent.

At first, Aethelbert thought Augustine would try to cast spells on him. But he soon changed his mind and became a Christian.

Augustine set up a monastery at Canterbury, in Kent, and became the first Archbishop of Canterbury – the Pope's most senior official in Britain. Many people in Kent and Essex (the East Saxons' kingdom) were soon converted, too.

Stormy relations

By the second half of the 7th century, there were monasteries and churches all over Britain. But the Irish and Roman Christians became locked in a bitter feud, as they disagreed over the right way to do things. Their long-running arguments finally came to a head when a huge row blew up over how to fix the date for Easter each year.

In 664, they held a meeting at Whitby Abbey to settle their differences. The Roman monks won the day, and Christians across Britain agreed to be guided by the teachings of the Pope in Rome.

These are the ruins of Whitby Abbey in Yorkshire. The first abbey here was founded in 657 by an Anglo-Saxon noblewoman named Hild. She oversaw the meeting at Whitby in the year 664.

Little angels

According to one story, Pope Gregory had his first sight of Anglo-Saxons at a slave market in Rome. The fair skin and hair of some young slaves made him exclaim that they were not *Angles*, but angels!

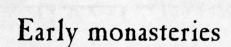

These beautifully decorated letters spell out a shortened version of the name *Christ*.

They are from the *Lindisfarne Gospels*, a gorgeous Christian book illustrated by a highly-skilled monk on the island of Lindisfarne. It was made around the year 700, and is now considered one of Britain's most valuable treasures.

The swirling designs were inspired by Celtic art.

Preaching crosses

Up and down Britain, people converted to Christianity faster than churches could be built. So stone crosses were put up to mark places of prayer and teaching.

These crosses were often decorated with religious scenes and texts.

Early monasteries

As Christianity took hold in 7th-century Britain, more and more monasteries were set up. They came in all shapes and sizes. Some were simple wooden buildings on remote islands or hills, while others were huge compounds containing churches, dormitories, workshops and farmland. The richest monasteries had impressive stone churches with glass windows. Glass was hugely expensive at the time.

Treasured books

Large monasteries had a room called a *scriptorium* where monks painstakingly copied out religious or educational texts into decorated books, known as *manuscripts*. Working in cold rooms, over a thousand years before electric lights were invented, this must have been slow, eye-straining work. But it was also considered an act of devotion to God, so books were incredibly valuable. They were kept safe in libraries.

A monk's life

Each monastery had its own set of rules about how its monks should live. These were laid down by the head monk, the Abbot.

But most monks did roughly the same things – they prayed several times a day, created manuscripts, studied and farmed their land. Some also taught the sons of nobles, giving them religious instruction and showing them how to read and write.

Wealthy people often gave money and land to monasteries. In return, the monks said prayers for their souls after they died. These donations made some monasteries very rich.

Cultural revolution

In 668, the Pope appointed a Greek scholar named Theodore to be Archbishop of Canterbury. Theodore, who was nearly 70, transformed the Church, giving it a clear structure. He also founded a school in Canterbury and gave classes on scripture, astronomy and poetry.

Under his guidance, there was a golden age of Anglo-Saxon learning. Some monasteries began to make elaborate manuscripts, with exquisite illustrations known as *illuminations*.

Monks and nuns

Many women devoted their lives to their religion too. They became nuns and lived in monastic communities, later known as nunneries. Some nunneries were even built next to monasteries, although the monks and nuns were strictly separated. Several of these 'double monasteries' were run by noblewomen who had become nuns, such as Hild, Abbess of Whitby.

Making books

To make a manuscript, monks had to do everything from making their own writing materials, to creating the illustrations that decorated the text.

They treated cow and sheep skins to create smooth sheets, known as *vellum*, or parchment.

They wrote with pens made from feathers, and ink made from trees. Then, they sewed up the pages into books.

The monks' parchment and ink were much longer-lasting than materials used for books today. Some manuscripts still exist.

Changes in the north

The kingdoms that had formed in the 6th century continued to change – especially in the north. There, the Celtic kingdom of Strathclyde and Pictish lands bordered the Anglo-Saxon kingdoms of Bernicia and Deira. The borders often shifted as these kingdoms fought one another for power or land.

This map shows the main kingdoms in northern Britain. Anglo-Saxon areas are darker green.

Feast for the poor

One story tells of how King Oswald had just sat down to a feast, when he heard there were hungry beggars outside. He ordered his food to be given to them, as well as the silver plate on which it was served.

Northern crossroads

Around 604, Aethelfrith, King of Bernicia, claimed Deira for himself, and drove out Edwin, the heir to the kingdom. After Aethelfrith's death, Edwin returned and took control of both kingdoms, which together became known as Northumbria.

Edwin pushed his borders west and south. But, in 633, the leaders of Mercia and Gwynedd launched a joint attack on Northumbria. Together, they killed Edwin and took over his kingdom.

A warrior and a Christian

After Edwin's death, Aethelfrith's son Oswald returned from where he had been living in exile. He fought off the occupying forces in Northumbria to became the new king. Oswald had been brought up in the monastery on Iona and was deeply religious. Under his influence, Northumbria quickly became the most Christian of all the Anglo-Saxon kingdoms.

Separation and reunion

When Oswald died in 642, the alliance of Bernicia and Deira fell apart. Then, in 651, Oswald's brother Oswy of Bernicia defeated the king of Deira and united the kingdoms once more.

This was the start of a union between the two kingdoms that was to last for centuries.

Kings over Britain

During the following decades, Northumbrian kings conquered lands from the Picts, Britons and other Anglo-Saxon kingdoms. Northumbria became the most powerful kingdom in Britain, and its kings were known as *Bretwalda*, or 'high leaders'. This meant they were the overlords of many other kings across Britain.

But, in 685, Oswy's son and successor died in a battle against the Picts. Northumbria was weakened, and it never quite recovered its old power. Instead, in the 8th century, an ambitious king from another Anglo-Saxon kingdom stepped forward to claim the title of 'Bretwalda' for himself...

This stone was carved by Picts. Some experts think it shows the battle of 685 between the Picts and Anglo-Saxons. The man falling down in the lower right corner may be Oswy's son, Ecgfrith, who died in this battle.

Bamburgh castle, in Bernicia, was originally a coastal fort, built long before the Anglo-Saxons arrived. It was taken over by Bernician kings, who used it as their base. This castle was built over the fort's ruins in the 11th century.

Born into a noble family, Guthlac spent his youth as a successful warrior.

But, after becoming discontented with a life of battle, he gave it all up to become a monk.

Two years later, he left his monastery to live alone. He became well-known for his holy lifestyle, and people flocked to see him.

After his death in 714, Guthlac was declared a saint.

The rise of Mercia

The kingdom of Mercia, in the Midlands, had always been strong. But under the reigns of two great 8th-century kings – first King Aethelbald, then King Offa – it became more powerful than ever before.

Exile, politics and a new king

In the early 700s, a noble named Aethelbald was exiled by King Ceolred of Mercia, his second cousin. Ceolred wasn't very popular, and may have feared that Aethelbald would launch a challenge for the kingship.

While in exile, Aethelbald visited a monk named Guthlac, who lived in desolate marshland. Guthlac was famous for his prophecies and healing powers, and many powerful men sought his advice. He persuaded his most influential visitors to back Aethelbald.

In 716, Ceolred died suddenly of a seizure during a feast. With the support he had gathered, Aethelbald returned to Mercia and declared himself king.

King of the South

Aethelbald also became overlord of some other Anglo-Saxon kingdoms, and their leaders gave him gifts and promises of service. But this wasn't enough for him. He started to act as if he owned these kingdoms himself. Soon he ruled over most of the southern Anglo-Saxon lands, and he gave himself a new title, 'King of the South Angles'.

He died in 757, and was succeeded by a noble named Beornred. But Beornred was soon chased off by the next great Mercian leader – King Offa.

Mercian treasure trove

In July 2009, in a field in Staffordshire (once part of Mercia), a treasure hunter named Terry Herbert discovered a huge Anglo-Saxon hoard. With items dating from as far back as the 7th century, it's the most spectacular collection of Anglo-Saxon treasure ever found – much larger even than that unearthed at Sutton Hoo.

Over 1,300 objects were uncovered, of which most were parts of weapons and war gear. Many were wrought in gold and silver by master craftsmen, and decorated with precious stones or animal designs. They may have been trophies collected from the battlefield by a victorious Mercian warrior, or even a member of the royal family.

An eagle sits at either end of this gold piece, and a fish is shown in the middle.

This piece formed part of the hilt, or handle, of a sword. It's made of gold and garnet.

A quote from the Bible is inscribed in Latin on this gold strip.

This helmet plate would have hung by the wearer's cheek.

Over the coming years, historians will study the finds to learn more about the Anglo-Saxons. Many think the discovery may reveal lots of exciting new things about the Anglo-Saxon age.

King Offa

This is part of Offa's Dyke, a massive earth wall along the boundary between England and Wales.

The dyke was finished during Offa's reign (757-796). At 8m (26ft) high, 20m (66ft) wide in places, it was so huge that although it's been worn down over centuries, sections still stand today.

Aethelbald had conquered much of the south, but Offa went even further. He expanded Mercia hugely by capturing even more land from nearby kings. In the end, he more or less took control of all the Anglo-Saxon kingdoms – except for Northumbria and Wessex (the West Saxon kingdom).

So that no one could challenge him, Offa had many of the lesser Anglo-Saxon kings killed and he stripped the others of their title of 'king'. He also tried hard to conquer the people of Wales, but they resisted fiercely. Their mountainous country made fighting hard and, eventually, Offa was forced to admit defeat.

Building barriers

Both Aethelbald and Offa had to be very organized to keep control of such large territories. They kept lots of written records, and came up with new ways of defending their land. They made it compulsory for all landowners to help them build new fortifications. Soon, defensive earth banks and ditches sprang up around Mercia's most important settlements.

The most impressive new fortification was a vast earth wall between Mercia and the Welsh kingdoms, built to prevent attacks from the Welsh side. Known as Offa's Dyke, much of it is still standing today.

Roman ways

Before Offa's reign, most people in Britain didn't use money. They just exchanged one kind of goods for another. But Offa decided to start producing coins, which had hardly been used in Britain since Roman times. And, just like the Roman emperors, Offa made sure that his new coins showed his portrait.

Offa was also very enthusiastic about strengthening the Church in his kingdom. He even created a new role for a third archbishop – in the Mercian town of Lichfield (the others were in Canterbury and York) – although this didn't survive long after he died.

Resistance to Mercia

Mercia was so powerful that the only kingdoms that managed to cling onto their independence were Wessex and Northumbria. But they too might eventually have been absorbed into the kingdom of Mercia, if it hadn't been for the emergence of a terrible new threat at the end of the 8th century: the Vikings.

New money

front

back

Here are both sides of a silver penny, issued by King Offa. His portrait is on the front. The back shows the name of the man who made it.

Offa also issued this gold coin, based on Middle Eastern coins brought to Britain by traders. Both sides are marked with Arabic writing.

front

back

The front of this coin is marked with a portrait of Offa's wife, Cynethryth. Her name is on the back.

Trade and culture

During the 8th century, trade was increasing all across Europe. Coins were now widely used, making buying and selling easier for everyone. People knew how much each coin was worth, so they could be sure they weren't being cheated. Carrying the small, light coins was also much simpler than exchanging goods for other goods that might be bulky or easily damaged.

A series of trading ports, where locals and foreign merchants could trade goods with one another, sprang up all around the coasts of northwest Europe and southeast England.

The Anglo-Saxons called them *wics*. This word is still part of some place names today, such as Sandwich on the south coast and Ipswich in the east. Other *wics* grew up at London, York and Southampton.

Men of letters

It wasn't just trade that was becoming more international. Cultural exchanges were taking place across Europe too. Latin had caught on as the language for most official business in Britain and much of Europe. This enabled educated Anglo-Saxons to communicate with people all over the continent.

Some Anglo-Saxons wrote to people all across Europe. Letters still survive that were sent between King Offa of Mercia and Emperor Charlemagne, who ruled over much of western Europe, including parts of what are now France, Germany and Italy.

Charlemagne also corresponded with Alcuin, an Anglo-Saxon scholar from York, whose fame for learning and wisdom had spread across Europe. In the end, Alcuin went to live at Charlemagne's court and became one of his most trusted advisers.

This is part of the opening page of a book completed in 731 by Bede, a Northumbrian monk and historian.

His history of England covered the period from the time of the Romans up to his own day.

Historians still rely on Bede's work today, although parts are now thought to be inaccurate.

Poetry and art

The Celtic Britons and Anglo-Saxons had a long tradition of composing poetry, which they passed on by word of mouth. Now, they began to write down more of their poetry.

Anglo-Saxon verses were often inspired by stories and styles from northern Europe. The most famous poem to survive is named *Beowulf* after its warrior hero, and tells the epic tale of his battles with monsters and a dragon.

Art was changing too, as different styles were brought together. Metalworkers, carvers and manuscript illustrators were combining delicate interlacing patterns, created by Celtic-speaking craftsmen, with bold Anglo-Saxon designs.

In the epic Anglo-Saxon poem, *Beowulf*, the hero fights a terrible marsh-monster named Grendel and kills it with his bare hands.

Celtic kingdoms

Across Britain, people were becoming more aware of their own distinct cultures. Thanks to monks and traders, people from Celtic-speaking regions – Ireland, Cornwall, Wales and Scotland – were in close contact with each other, but their languages were becoming more different.

Each of these regions was still made up of smaller kingdoms. But, just as several Anglo-Saxon kingdoms had merged to form Northumbria, some of these Celtic kingdoms were beginning to join together to form bigger kingdoms.

This brooch was made from silver, gold and amber in around 700. It was probably designed by Scottish metalworkers, who used techniques and designs from Scotland, Ireland and England to stunning effect.

Shown here at two-thirds its real size, this brooch was clearly designed to make a big impact and may even have belonged to a Scots king.

Raiders from the sea

This scene shows a Viking raid on a monastery. The raiders stole valuable objects, captured or killed the locals, and destroyed buildings.

Around 789, three long, low ships appeared off the coast of Wessex. As they came into shore, the local official rode out to greet the newcomers. But the men from the ships struck him down at once and killed him.

This was only the first in a series of bloody raids. The attackers stripped settlements of valuables, killed anyone who stood in their way and then sailed off.

These fearsome raiders were warriors known as Vikings. They came from areas that are now part of Norway, Denmark and Sweden. For the next 60 years or so, shiploads of Vikings arrived in the spring and summer to seize everything they could carry away on their boats. When they left, they often burned or destroyed anything they couldn't take with them.

People didn't know how to fight off the Vikings. It was no good gathering an army, as no one knew where or when the next raid might strike. Instead, they prayed for help, but this didn't seem to make any difference either.

In fact, the Vikings often targeted churches and monasteries for their precious ornaments, killing the monks and burning their libraries. Some people thought God was punishing them.

From bad to worse

Then, in 851, things changed. For the first time, the Vikings didn't sail away after the summer. Instead, they camped near their ships for the winter, living off the spoils of their summer raids. That way, they were in place for the next round of raids in the spring. It wasn't long before they decided to stay for good.

By the mid-860s, the Vikings were starting to conquer Britain. A huge army of Danish Vikings landed in 865. Within five years, they had taken over Northumbria and East Anglia, weakened the once-powerful kingdom of Mercia, and were preparing to attack Wessex.

At the same time, a band of Vikings from Norway was attacking the northwest coast of Scotland, the Western Isles, Orkney, Shetland, and parts of Ireland.

Despite strong resistance, in just a few years, the Vikings had conquered much of Britain.

King Edmund of East Anglia was captured by Vikings in 869. One legend describes how they tied him to a tree, fired arrows at him, then beheaded him.

The King's remains were eventually laid to rest at an abbey called Bury St. Edmunds.

These metal heads of Viking weapons were found in London. The wooden handles are modern as the original ones decomposed long ago.

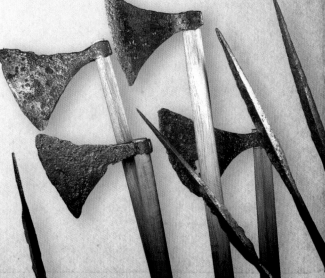

The Vikings

The lands that the Vikings came from were criss-crossed by rivers and lakes, and bordered by seas. Surrounded by all this water, it's hardly surprising they became master shipbuilders and navigators.

Many Viking warships had dragon heads like this one at the front, to scare their enemies.

By the 9th century, the Vikings were seeking new places to live, possibly after outgrowing their own homelands. They struck out across Europe, Africa and Asia, and the most intrepid of them even reached North America. Many modern place names are reminders of their travels – Greenland was named by Viking explorers, and Russia gets its name from a tribe of Vikings called the Rus.

Sailing the seas

The designs for Viking ships had been perfected by generations of expert shipbuilders. Their fast, streamlined ships were made from wooden planks held together by iron rivets, and coated with tar from pine trees.

Viking warships, called *longships*, could be sailed up rivers to attack towns and villages inland.

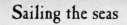

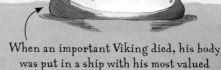

When an important Viking died, his body was put in a ship with his most valued treasures. Then the ship was buried or sent out to sea, sometimes in flames.

Merchant ships, called *knorrs*, had a pit in the middle to hold goods.

Warrior gods

Although the Vikings and Anglo-Saxons were enemies, they had much in common.

The Vikings were pagans, and their religion, based on many war-like gods, was very similar to the one the Anglo-Saxons had followed before they became Christians. Vikings were fearless fighters because they believed that those who died in battle were promised entrance into a special paradise.

Kings and warlords

The Vikings were as efficient as they were ferocious. Their armies could cover large distances swiftly, using longships to navigate rivers, and horses to cover land.

Viking troops were also well-organized and often had brilliant leaders, such as the warrior-kings Ivar and Halfdan. Some legends say they were the sons of a Danish king who terrorized western Europe before being captured, tortured and killed by the king of Northumbria in 865.

These stories tell that, with his dying words, the Danish king threatened that his sons would seek vengeance for his death. The very next year, Ivar and Halfdan plundered Northumbria and killed its king.

Merchants and traders

But Vikings didn't just set out to conquer new lands. Many were merchants, and their trade routes covered much of the world. They carried furs, slaves and amber east to trade in the huge, bustling city of Constantinople (now Istanbul) and they crossed deserts to reach the Arabian city of Baghdad. Then they returned laden with silver, spices, silk and other luxury goods.

Viking gods

The Vikings believed in many gods and goddesses. Here are some of the main ones:

Odin was the ruler of the gods. He rode an eight-legged horse.

Thor was the god of thunder. He carried a hammer, and drove a chariot pulled by goats.

Freya was the goddess of love and death. She wore a cloak made of falcon feathers, and her chariot was drawn by cats.

Alfred the Great

Prayers and war

King Ethelred was very religious. According to one story, the Vikings began an attack before he had finished saying his prayers. But Ethelred would not be interrupted. Instead, his brother Alfred had to take over and lead his troops into battle.

Having conquered Northumbria, East Anglia and much of Mercia, the Viking raiders now turned their attentions to Wessex.

One cold day in January 871, the Viking army was poised to attack. King Ethelred of Wessex rode out to meet them, accompanied by his forces and his younger brother, Alfred. The Vikings won this first battle, but the Wessex forces soon gained a victory of their own. This was to be just the start of a long struggle between them.

Disaster strikes

In the spring of 871, Ethelred died and was succeeded by Alfred. At the same time, Viking reinforcements arrived from Denmark. Alfred spent a year on the losing side of skirmishes. Eventually he gave in, and was forced to pay the Viking army not to attack Wessex again.

In 876, a Danish leader called Guthrum led yet another Viking attack on Wessex. This time, Alfred managed to drive them away. But, less than two years later, Guthrum launched a surprise attack on Alfred's camp, where the king and his followers were relaxing after their Christmas celebrations. The Wessex forces were caught off-guard, and many were killed. Alfred himself only just managed to escape.

This photograph shows the Somerset marshes. Here, Alfred hid to escape the Vikings. He made a fort on an island called Athelney, to use as his base. Later, he built an abbey on the same site.

Turn of the tide

Alfred spent several desperate months hiding out in the marshes, with only a few followers. But he worked tirelessly to gather support. By May, he was ready to take on the Vikings again. He built up an army, and set off to face Guthrum's troops.

It was the Vikings' turn to be caught unawares. They lost the battle that followed, and surrendered two weeks later. Alfred agreed peace terms, on the condition that Guthrum became a Christian.

Guthrum promised not to attack Wessex again, while Alfred accepted that the Vikings had settled for good. The leaders also set a boundary between Alfred's land to the west, and the Vikings' territory to the east.

Standing strong

Alfred knew that the peace wouldn't last. So he swiftly reorganized his army into a better fighting unit, ordered a huge fleet of ships, and built a series of fortified towns. These tactics paid off. Wessex withstood all future Viking attacks, and Alfred even reclaimed London for the Anglo-Saxons.

Other Anglo-Saxon leaders began to look to Alfred for leadership too, and to future generations he became known as Alfred the Great.

Undercover king

A legend tells of how Alfred met a peasant woman while in hiding. Not knowing who he was, she asked him to watch some cakes she was cooking. But Alfred was thinking about how to save his kingdom, and let the cakes burn.

When the woman came back, she scolded Alfred. Some versions of the tale say that when she found out who he was, she tried to apologize. But Alfred humbly said that he was the one who should say sorry.

Alfred the scholar

Like many Anglo-Saxons at the time, Alfred thought the Viking attacks were God's way of punishing them for not being good enough Christians. So he dedicated himself to encouraging his people to be more devout, as a way of pleasing God and preventing further attacks.

It didn't help that the Vikings had destroyed many monasteries, slaughtering the educated monks and burning their libraries. By Alfred's time, there were hardly any Anglo-Saxons left who could read at all.

So he brought in scholars from overseas, began to rebuild the monasteries and commissioned new books. He also had other works translated into English, and even wrote some of the best translations himself. These included 50 psalms and a work by Pope Gregory about how priests should act.

The rise of the English

The nobles of what remained of Mercia had accepted Alfred as their overlord, but they didn't want their lands to be merged into his kingdom. Alfred knew he'd have to tread carefully if he wanted Wessex's authority in Mercia to last. He allowed the Mercians to keep their own leader, Ethelred. But Alfred also arranged for his daughter, Aethelflaed, to marry Ethelred, so it was obvious that real power lay with Wessex.

Alfred decided that it was wisest to draw attention to what united the Anglo-Saxons, rather than what divided them. He encouraged people to read and write in English, the language they shared (rather than Latin), and to take pride in their common culture.

This focus on 'Englishness' brought the Anglo-Saxons together. They began to call themselves *Angelcynn* – the English.

This is probably the handle of a pointer, used to follow words while reading. Writing around the edge reads 'Alfred ordered me made' in Old English. It was found buried near Athelney.

Alfred's histories

Scholars who probably lived at Alfred's court wrote an account of Anglo-Saxon history. Then copies were sent far and wide, so future events could be added as they happened. These records were brought together later, and are called the *Anglo-Saxon Chronicle*.

Danish England

The lands the Vikings had occupied became known as the Danelaw, because they imposed Danish laws and customs there. The settlers made their capital in the northern city of Eoforwic, which they renamed *Jorvik* – modern-day York.

They split the Midlands into areas based around five strongholds: Leicester, Nottingham, Lincoln, Stamford and Derby, later known as the Five Boroughs.

As the Anglo-Saxons had done centuries earlier, the Danish Vikings soon settled down to live as farmers. They gave Danish names to the places where they lived, many of which survive today – including those ending in *thwaite*, *ness*, *thorpe* and *by*.

Taking over the fight

In 899, Alfred died and his son, Edward, became King of Wessex. Meanwhile, what remained of Mercia was ruled by Ethelred and Aethelflaed, Edward's sister. All three worked together to reclaim land from the Vikings.

Ethelred died in 911. Aethelflaed, a great warrior queen, defended Mercia and led attacks on the Danelaw until her death in 918. Then Edward declared himself King in Mercia, which was never independent again.

By the time Edward died in 924, he had conquered the Danelaw up to the Humber river, including the Five Boroughs, although the settlers in this part of the Danelaw kept their own customs.

Alfred is remembered as the greatest Anglo-Saxon king. This statue of him was put up in Winchester, his main base, a thousand years after his death.

This cemetery on the Scottish island of Iona was the burial place for many early Scottish kings, including Kenneth MacAlpin.

Destiny's stone

A flat piece of rock called the Stone of Destiny was used in king-making ceremonies in the new Scottish kingdom of Alba. Before that, it was probably used by Pictish kings. Some legends even trace it back to the Bible.

United kingdoms?

The Viking raids had hit every corner of the British Isles, and had brought much bloodshed. But they also sowed early seeds of unity within the different regions.

Picts and Scots

For centuries, the most northerly part of Britain had been home to two main groups: the Picts and the Scots. To their south was Strathclyde – a kingdom of Britons, which today is part of Scotland.

A Scots king called Constantin MacFergus gained control over the Picts in the late 8th century. But his dynasty didn't last, partly because of Viking raids.

Then, around 850, another Scots king, Kenneth MacAlpin, brought the Picts and Scots under a single rule once more. His subjects were drawn together by their struggle against the Vikings, and under his descendants, this kingdom became known as Alba. It formed the core of what later became Scotland.

Divided Wales

At the same time, Wales was made up of separate kingdoms, the most powerful of which was Gwynedd.

From the 840s, the King of Gwynedd, Rhodri *Mawr*, 'the Great', came to rule most of Wales – through marriage, inheritance and probably conquest, too. But when he died, his kingdom was split between his three sons – which was the custom in Wales.

Just under a century later, most of Wales was again united under Rhodri's grandson Hywel *Dda*, 'the Good'. But his kingdom was broken up after his death too, and Wales remained divided for another century.

Making laws

The first Welsh laws were written down during Hywel Dda's reign. After his death, Hywel was remembered as a lawmaker.

Viking Ireland

Ireland was divided into kingdoms interspersed with Viking settlements, which included the prosperous town of Dublin. In 917, a new wave of Norwegian Vikings attacked, led by two warriors named Sihtric and Ragnall. They took charge in Dublin, which Sihtric used as a base to launch attacks on the rest of Ireland.

Then Ragnall sailed to Britain and took over Viking Northumbria, making his base in Jorvik. His authority reached down to the Humber river. Further south, the rest of the Danelaw remained under King Edward's control.

When Ragnall died in 920, Sihtric became King in Jorvik and another Viking, named Guthfrith, became King in Dublin.

This map shows some of the main kingdoms and cities in the 10th century.

~ Boundary agreed by Alfred and Guthrum

● Norwegian Viking cities

● 'Five Boroughs' of the Danish Vikings

● Anglo-Saxon settlements

ALBA

STRATHCLYDE

NORTHUMBRIA

Jorvik ● Humber river

IRELAND

Dublin ●

GWYNEDD

DANELAW   ● Lincoln

POWYS

Derby ● ● Nottingham

● Stamford

Leicester

Cork ●

DYFED

MERCIA

WESSEX   London ●

Athelney ●   ● Winchester

Athelstan of England

In 925, Alfred the Great's grandson, Athelstan, was crowned King of the English. At first, his kingdom stretched no further north than the Humber river.

But Athelstan proved to be just as great as his grandfather, and he seized the northern part of the Danelaw, Northumbria, from the Vikings. This made him the very first king of all of England.

King and overlord

When Athelstan first became king, he agreed a peace treaty with Sihtric, the Viking king in Jorvik. But when Sihtric died in early 927, Athelstan threw Sihtric's young son out of Jorvik, and took control of Northumbria for himself.

In July that year, Athelstan met several British leaders, including King Constantine of Alba and King Owain of Strathclyde. They recognized him as their overlord, and he began to call himself 'King of Britain'.

Athelstan also became the overlord of Hywel Dda, ruler of much of Wales. They reached a peaceful settlement about their borders, and Hywel often visited the English king. But Athelstan's relations with Constantine and Owain seem to have deteriorated.

This picture from Athelstan's reign shows him presenting a manuscript to a religious community.

Like his grandfather, Alfred, Athelstan knew the importance of learning, and he gave generously to churches.

The battle that shaped Britain

In 934, Athelstan's troops invaded Strathclyde and then struck Alba. They only left once Athelstan's authority was beyond question.

But Constantine soon planned his revenge. He joined forces with the Vikings in Ireland and Britons in Strathclyde, and in 937 they marched against Athelstan. The two sides met at the Battle of Brunanburh – a massive clash, during which both sides suffered terrible losses. It was reported that two of Athelstan's cousins died in the bloodbath, and Constantine even lost his son.

Eventually, Athelstan emerged victorious and was again proclaimed overlord of Britain. But he never again had sufficient forces to expand his lands further.

"The field was sodden with warriors' blood... Never before was there more slaughter on this island; never so many people killed by the sword's edge..."

This comes from a poem in the *Anglo-Saxon Chronicle*, which describes the epic Battle of Brunanburh.

Northumbrian struggles

Athelstan died just two years later, and was succeeded by his half-brothers: first Edmund, and then Eadred. Both had to contend with the Irish Vikings, who returned time and again to reclaim Jorvik. But, by the end of Eadred's reign, the Vikings had been defeated for good. After that, Northumbria remained a permanent part of England.

This is a reenactment of an Anglo-Saxon battle. Warriors had round shields and sharp spears, and the richest of them had swords.

Viking York

Even after the Viking rulers were defeated, many Viking settlers stayed in England. They lived peacefully in the Danelaw under English rule, while still keeping their old customs and way of life. Viking influence was especially strong in Jorvik.

The Vikings soon became Christians, but didn't quite give up their old ways and beliefs.

This stone cross, with a traditional armed Viking warrior carved on it, was made by Danish Christian converts in Yorkshire.

A Viking fortress

Once a royal Anglo-Saxon town, and before that a Roman fort, Jorvik became the Vikings' capital in the 9th century. They repaired the Roman walls, created new fortifications, and built rows of houses. Even when Jorvik came under English rule in the 10th century, life there didn't change much.

Digging up the past

New buildings were later built over Jorvik. So there's a huge number of Viking remains still to be discovered – mostly buried beneath the modern city of York.

Every so often, historians get a chance to find out what's hidden. In the 1970s, two buildings on the street of Coppergate were demolished. Experts were able to investigate the site before new building began, but they had no idea of the scale of what awaited them...

This shows what Jorvik may have looked like in the 10th century. Goods are being brought to the bustling town on ships.

Jorvik life

The Coppergate dig revealed part of a Jorvik street from the 10th century, complete with Viking houses, yards and even human remains. The discoveries, well-preserved in rich, damp soil, gave an amazingly detailed impression of the lives of Jorvik citizens.

The houses were long and thin, and tightly packed together. At the back of each, there was a narrow strip of land which usually had a workshop or warehouse, a well, a waste heap and toilet, and space to keep poultry or livestock. Inside, the houses had earth floors, hearths, areas for sleeping and places to sit.

Trade and industry

Remnants of so many different kinds of crafts were uncovered that it's likely that Jorvik was home to many skilled manufacturers. The fronts of the houses probably served as shops, where people could buy goods such as clothing, ornaments and knives.

The customers weren't all local, either – buyers came from all over Europe to trade with the Jorvik craftsmen. Many left behind evidence of their visits. Tools from as far away as Norway and Denmark were found, as well as silk from Byzantium and coins from what is now Uzbekistan.

Shopping street

These goods were for sale in and around Coppergate:

Beads, rings and necklaces

Textiles and clothing

Brooches, pins and buckles

Pots

Leather shoes

Wooden bowls and cups

Coppergate means 'street of the cup-makers' in the Vikings' language, Old Norse.

One side of this coin shows King Edgar's portrait, and the other shows where it was made.

Before King Edgar's rule, different areas had their own coins. But he introduced a single currency for the whole kingdom.

Edgar the Peaceful

In 959, Athelstan's nephew, Edgar, became King of England. His 16-year reign was a time of peace within the kingdom, and free of Viking attacks. Because of this, he is often known as Edgar the Peaceful. But the years before his reign had been more troubled.

A storm before the calm

Four years before Edgar came to the throne, his older brother Eadwig had become king. He had cast off his predecessor's advisers, and replaced many of them with his own relatives – a policy which made him very unpopular with lots of nobles.

In 957, Mercian and Northumbrian noble families joined forces to rebel against King Eadwig. They insisted on being governed by Edgar instead. With Eadwig still ruling over the south, England was effectively split into two.

Eadwig died in 959 with no children, so Edgar was the natural choice to succeed him as king. A crisis was averted and the kingdom was united once more.

One legend describes how Eadwig left his coronation feast to spend time with two women. He was rebuked by an abbot named Dunstan, who he furiously banished.

Edgar later recalled Dunstan, and made him Archbishop of Canterbury.

The peacemaker

Once Edgar was king, things calmed down. He was a strong ruler, who was prepared to use force in order to keep the peace. One of the only rebellions of his reign took place in 970 on the island of Thanet, off the coast of Kent. Edgar swiftly sent in troops, who quashed the troublemakers and seized anything of value from the land.

In fact, it's likely that Edgar's nickname – *pacificus* in Latin – really meant not 'peaceful', but 'peacemaker'.

Shows of power

In 973, Edgar was crowned in a grand ceremony at
Bath. This was conducted in a religious manner, to
suggest he was God's choice for King. A variation of it
is still used when British monarchs are crowned today.

After Bath, he is said to have staged an event near
Chester, where he was rowed along the river Dee by
other British rulers. He steered the boat, showing his
power over the others.

Several lesser British
kings are said to have
rowed Edgar along the
river in Chester. They
included Kenneth II of
Scotland, Jacob of
Gywnedd and Dunmail
of Strathclyde.

Reformation and resentment

But secretly, many nobles were unhappy. Edgar
wanted to reform the monasteries, as many had become
corrupt. Head monks usually came from rich families,
who often treated the monasteries' land as their own.

Edgar supported Church leaders who introduced
tighter rules for monks, and he made large areas of
Church land independent from nobles. Lots of nobles
were furious, but no one dared complain.

This illustration from
966 shows King Edgar
flanked by two saints, to
make a point of his
closeness to God.

These are the ruins of Corfe Castle, in Dorset, which is near the site of the murder of King Edward, Edgar's older son.

Troubled times

When Edgar died in 975, the trouble that had been brewing during his reign finally came to a head. Some nobles supported his reforms of the monasteries, but others were violently opposed to them. The two sides came to blows, as several landowners seized back land that Edgar had granted to the monasteries, but which they believed belonged to them.

Evil step-mother

King Edward was murdered while he was visiting his half-brother Ethelred, who had been staying near Corfe with his mother, Aelfthryth.

Later accounts claimed that Aelfthryth herself was involved in the plot. Some say she offered Edward a drink as he arrived, distracting him while the murderer stabbed him from behind.

An heir too many

It didn't help that Edgar had two sons by different wives. Some nobles wanted the elder son, Edward, to be king. He was 12, and would soon be old enough to start ruling for himself. Others backed the younger son, Ethelred, who was 9. His mother, Aelfthryth, helped to gather supporters for him.

After much disagreement, Edward succeeded his father. But events got out of hand just three years later, when Edward was killed by Ethelred's supporters.

All the king's men

People all over England were outraged by Edward's murder, and he became known as Edward the Martyr. Ethelred became king, but his rule was marred by his connection to the murderers. And, as he was still only 12, he had to rely on his supporters to run the country for him, in particular his mother Aelfthryth.

But when he was old enough to govern for himself, Ethelred turned out to be a weak king. He cast out his old advisers, picking new ones who greedily persuaded him to do whatever was best for themselves.

A new Viking threat

Meanwhile, Vikings from Denmark and Norway resumed their raids along the southern English coastline. At first, these attacks were fairly small-scale.

But in 991, a massive fleet of Viking longships set sail, heading for England. Things were about to go from bad to worse.

Unready, unraed

Ethelred is often called *the Unready*. Some people think this is because he failed to cope with the Vikings. But actually it's from an early nickname *Ethelred Unraed*, meaning Ethelred the ill-Advised.

This is a reconstruction of a Viking longship. According to the *Anglo-Saxon Chronicle*, in 991 the Viking fleet was made up of 93 ships like this.

The Battle of Maldon

In August 991, the Viking forces landed on an island off the east coast of England, near Maldon, in Essex. An English army had massed to face them on the mainland, led by battle veteran Ealdorman Bryhtnoth of Essex.

According to a poem written soon after, the water between the English and Vikings was too wide for them to exchange any more than words and arrows. So the raiders asked permission to cross a causeway linking the island to the mainland in safety. Byrhtnoth agreed – maybe because he wanted a fair fight, or maybe just to stop the Vikings from sailing off to strike elsewhere.

Once the Vikings crossed the causeway, there was a fierce battle in which Byrhtnoth was killed. The poem describes how many of his men fled to save their lives, but the bravest remained to fight. Despite the efforts of Byrhtnoth's loyal men, the Vikings won the battle.

The site of the Battle of Maldon

Normandy, where Vikings took refuge

This picture shows Byrhtnoth, aged around 60, leading his troops (on the left) into battle at Maldon. During the fight, he was beheaded by the Vikings. Centuries later, the headless skeleton of a man who had been over 2m tall (around 6 feet 9 inches) was unearthed. Experts think this was probably Byrhtnoth's body.

A new ally

After this defeat, Ethelred paid the Vikings to leave. But he also looked for other ways to keep them away.

Previously, the Vikings had often sheltered in Normandy in France, where Viking descendants called the Normans had settled. To try to stop this, Ethelred had made a peace treaty with the Duke of Normandy. After Maldon, this pact was more vital than ever, and in 1002 Ethelred strengthened it by marrying the Duke's sister, Emma.

Drastic measures

Even so, the Viking raids continued. Ethelred had to keep taxing his people to raise money to pay off the invaders, and as a result, his popularity plummeted.

In November 1002, at the end of his tether, Ethelred ordered the murder of all Danes in England – even those who'd been living there peacefully for decades. The massacre is said to have enraged King Swein of Denmark, who swiftly attacked.

Viking demands

No matter how much Ethelred paid the Vikings, they kept coming back. And each time, he had to pay them even more to leave.

In 991, they demanded £10,000.

In 994 they demanded £16,000.

In 1002, they demanded £24,000.

Chaos and conquest

Swein and his forces had been raiding England for years, wreaking destruction wherever they went. But eventually, he decided that he wanted to conquer England, rather than simply raiding it.

In the summer of 1013, he set sail with his son, Canute, and a large Danish fleet. They sailed up the Humber, and landed in the north of England.

The weary English were no match for Swein. He was quickly accepted as king in the Danelaw (the area the Vikings had first occupied during Alfred's time), and by 1014, he had conquered the whole of England. Ethelred, Emma and their children fled to Normandy.

Short-lived reign

Swein died just a few months later, in February 1014. His elder son, Harald, succeeded him in Denmark, while Canute was declared King of England by the Danish army. He soon gained support in the north – the old heartland of the Danelaw.

Terms and conditions

Meanwhile, English nobles in the south invited Ethelred to return as king. But he had been so unpopular, thanks to his heavy taxes and disastrous handling of the Viking attacks, that he was only allowed to come back if he promised to treat his subjects better than before.

Humiliated but determined to take back what he believed was his, Ethelred agreed. In spring 1014, he returned to England, and turned his attention to driving out the Danes. He caught them unprepared and managed to force Canute back to Denmark.

This is the only surviving Viking helmet. It's from the 10th century, and was found in Norway.

"We richly deserve the misery that we're suffering, and we must work hard to please God if things are going to start getting better."

Archbishop Wulfstan of York said this in a sermon in 1014. He believed that the suffering caused by the Vikings' return was a punishment from God.

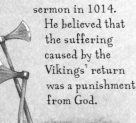

A family affair

Even with Canute gone, Ethelred faced problems at home. Many people in the north hadn't forgiven his massacre of the Danes, and lots had supported Swein and Canute. Their anger flared up early in 1015, with a huge rebellion, led by Ethelred's own son Edmund. He was protesting against corruption in his father's court. By the summer, Edmund was widely accepted as the ruler in the north.

Then, in August, Canute invaded. Edmund led the resistance, and was far more successful than his father had ever been. When Ethelred died in April 1016, Edmund succeeded him. He soon became known as 'Edmund Ironside' for his strength and courage.

Stalemate and succession

After months of fighting, Canute finally won a major victory in October 1016. But so many of his men were killed that he couldn't go on fighting, so he agreed to split the kingdom with Edmund. The pair also agreed that when one died, the other would inherit his land.

This agreement probably wouldn't have lasted, but Edmund died just a month later, and Canute became King of all England.

Treachery

In these dangerous times it was difficult to know who to trust.

One ambitious earl, named Eadric Streona, started out as Ethelred's adviser, but switched sides several times, hoping to gain power by backing the winner.

One story tells how, while supposedly fighting for Edmund, Eadric switched to Canute's side, and even beheaded a soldier who looked like Edmund.

This aerial photograph shows the outlines of a coastal fort built in Denmark in the late 10th century. It's one of several similar forts, constructed by powerful Danish kings to house their armies.

King Canute

Canute had become King of England through battle and bloodshed. Yet his reign proved to be prosperous and, in the end, peaceful.

But to start with, things weren't easy.

Early years

The English had suffered heavily during decades of Viking raids, so Canute was deeply unpopular. He became even more disliked when he had to tax his new subjects to raise the money he needed to pay his army.

To prevent an uprising, he divided England into four regions – Wessex, Mercia, Northumbria and East Anglia. He kept control of Wessex and put three of his earls in charge of the others, where they kept a close watch for trouble. A few years later, Canute passed control of Wessex to an Englishman named Godwine.

Building bridges

But Canute knew that to be a successful king, he'd have to win over his new subjects. In 1017, he married Ethelred's widow, Emma, to smooth the transition from English to Danish rule. He also gave generously to the Church, and brought back the laws of Edgar the Peaceful.

This brooch was made in England, but it shows twisting animals that are typical of Viking art. Scandivanian styles like this became popular in England around the time of Canute.

This illustration of Canute appears in a manuscript made during his lifetime. It shows him with his wife Emma, presenting a cross to a monastery in Winchester.

Building an empire

A few years after becoming King of England, Canute's brother died and he became King of Denmark. Soon after, he conquered parts of Sweden and Norway too. Canute's territories now made up an empire that covered the lands of those who had once raided England. This meant he could prevent further attacks – to the relief of the exhausted English.

    After several skirmishes with Scotland, Canute also reached an agreement with the Scots king, Malcolm II, in which both promised peace and friendship.

A pact for peace

Once it was clear that Canute's rule would be peaceful, the English came to accept him. He was often away in Scandinavia, but sent back several letters that were read out to the English public, promising them peace and protection in return for their loyalty. It seemed to be a deal that both sides were happy to keep.

The king's army

Canute dismissed most of his army in 1018. But he kept a small force, made up of professional warriors known as *housecarls*.

A messy succession

In 1035, Canute died, and the peace his reign had brought came to an abrupt end. Disputes over who should succeed him led to a crisis that threatened to spark a civil war.

Succession struggles

Canute had wanted his lands to pass to his son Harthacanute. But, by the time he died, his empire was failing. His Norwegian lands had broken away, and their king, Magnus, wanted control of Denmark too. Busy defending his Danish lands, Harthacanute didn't have time to go to England to be crowned.

Many English nobles were wary of making Harthacanute king while he was overseas, so they invited Harold, another of Canute's sons, to rule until Harthacanute arrived. Eventually, they gave up on Harthacanute and crowned Harold instead.

It was 1039 before Harthacanute could leave Denmark to claim England for himself. Another battle for the crown seemed to be looming. But, by the time Harthacanute arrived, Harold had fallen ill and died. Harthacanute was accepted as king soon after.

Reunited brothers

One of Harthacanute's first acts as king was to order Harold's body to be dug up and thrown into a bog.

But he was much kinder to his last surviving half-brother, Edward, son of Ethelred and Emma.

Edward had grown up in exile in Normandy, but now he was invited to return to England.

When Harthacanute died in 1042, Edward succeeded him as King of England.

This picture shows Queen Emma being given a book, while her sons Harthacanute and Edward look on.

Harthacanute died on June 8, 1042, while still in his early twenties.

Accounts say that he suddenly dropped dead after taking a drink at a wedding feast. No one knows why he died – some thought he drank himself to death.

56

Earl on the rise

Edward was popular with ordinary people. But he never got on well with his nobles, particularly the ambitious Earl Godwine of Wessex.

Since being given control over Wessex by Canute, Godwine's power and influence had grown steadily. In 1036, he had been involved in the murder of Edward's brother, Alfred. By Edward's reign, Godwine was as powerful as the king, and Edward had no choice but to make him an ally by marrying his daughter, Edith.

As time passed, Edward had less and less to do with the running of his country, leaving it up to his nobles. He was happiest with his Norman friends, and spent most of his time hunting, praying and overseeing the construction of Westminster Abbey.

Saintly Edward

After he died, Edward was remembered as a deeply religious king. He became known as Edward *the Confessor* – confessor is a name given to someone who lived a holy life.

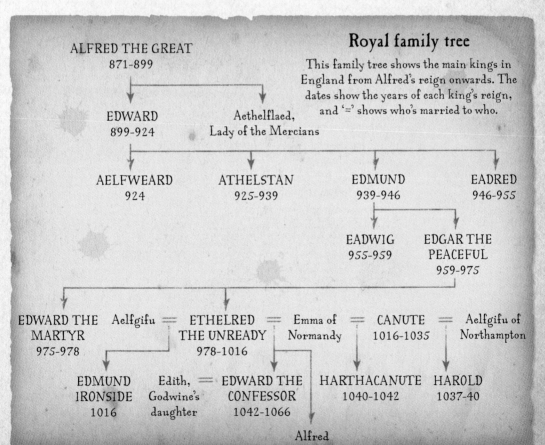

Royal family tree

This family tree shows the main kings in England from Alfred's reign onwards. The dates show the years of each king's reign, and '=' shows who's married to who.

ALFRED THE GREAT
871-899

EDWARD
899-924

Aethelflaed,
Lady of the Mercians

AELFWEARD
924

ATHELSTAN
925-939

EDMUND
939-946

EADRED
946-955

EADWIG
955-959

EDGAR THE
PEACEFUL
959-975

EDWARD THE
MARTYR
975-978

Aelfgifu

ETHELRED
THE UNREADY
978-1016

Emma of
Normandy

CANUTE
1016-1035

Aelfgifu of
Northampton

EDMUND
IRONSIDE
1016

Edith,
Godwine's
daughter

EDWARD THE
CONFESSOR
1042-1066

HARTHACANUTE
1040-1042

HAROLD
1037-40

Alfred

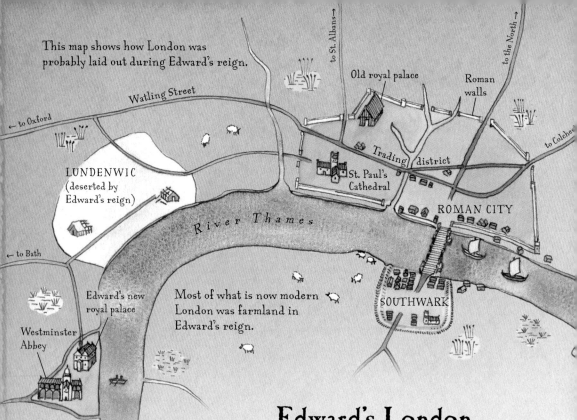

This map shows how London was probably laid out during Edward's reign.

to St. Albans →

to the North →

Old royal palace

Roman walls

Watling Street

← to Oxford

to Colchester →

LUNDENWIC
(deserted by
Edward's reign)

Trading district

St. Paul's
Cathedral

ROMAN CITY

River Thames

← to Bath

SOUTHWARK

Edward's new
royal palace

Most of what is now modern
London was farmland in
Edward's reign.

Westminster
Abbey

WESTMINSTER

Edward's London

Before Edward's reign, English kings had spent most
of their time moving from place to place, meeting with
their advisers and making laws as they went. But,
under Edward, London – and his new building project,
Westminster – became a kind of new 'capital', where
important government matters were dealt with.

Lost city

There's very little left
today to show what
London may have
looked like in Edward's
reign. Most of the
buildings were wooden
so have rotted away.

Even the few stone
buildings – mostly
churches – have been
rebuilt since. So there's
hardly anything of
those left either.

A ghost town

London had been through many changes before
Edward's reign. Originally a walled Roman city, it had
lain empty for years after the Anglo-Saxon invasions.
The Germanic settlers were farmers with no use for
grand Roman buildings, and may even have thought
the deserted ruins were haunted. Instead, they set up
villages outside the walls, including one which
eventually became a busy port called Lundenwic.

Once the Anglo-Saxons became Christians, some kings set up homes within the old Roman walls and, in 604, St. Paul's Cathedral was founded in the west of the city. But, on the whole, the area within the walls remained mostly deserted.

Retreat into the city

It wasn't until Vikings invaded in the 9th century that London really started to become a bustling city again. King Alfred realized the value of the sturdy Roman walls, and 'refounded' the city within them. He laid out a network of new streets, and oversaw the building of a fortified town, called 'Southwark', south of the river.

London continued to grow, in population and importance. By Edward's reign, it had become a thriving trading port.

Royal residence

Edward poured huge amounts of time and money into building a magnificent abbey and a royal palace in London. But he chose a site well outside the city walls. No longer fearing attacks from raiders, he picked an isolated marshy island over a mile and a half from the city. The abbey was known as 'Westminster' – the *minster*, or church, to the west of the city.

Edward's move west split London in two. The former Roman city became a hub of trade and commerce, while the royal court at Westminster was the main area of government. This division held true for centuries. Even today, Britain's central government is still based in Westminster, while the financial district is based in the east, in what used to be the Roman city.

St. Paul's

St. Paul's Cathedral, a great London landmark, has been through many changes since it was first built in the 7th century.

The earliest wooden church may have been destroyed by pagans. The next church burned down in 962. Its successor also caught fire in 1087.

Since then, the cathedral has been rebuilt in stone, twice.

SIC PORTATUR CORPVS EADWARDI REGIS AD ECCLESIAM S PETRI A

This embroidered picture shows Edward's body being carried to Westminster Abbey.

It comes from the Bayeux Tapestry, which depicts the events that led up to the Norman Conquest.

End of an era

Edward knew that he would be the last of Alfred's line to rule, as he had no children or close male relatives on his father's side. The ageing king also knew that there would be a terrible fight after he died if he didn't name a successor. So, in 1051, he chose his distant cousin, William, Duke of Normandy, as his heir.

Burying the hatchet

But, over a decade later, Edward was still alive. During this time, his enemy, Earl Godwine, had died and been succeeded in Wessex by his son, Harold Godwinson.

Harold was everything Edward had never been. Popular, witty and a successful army leader, he soon established himself as the chief among Edward's noblemen. By the time Edward died in January 1066, Harold had already taken over much of the running of the country. He seemed the obvious choice to become the next king.

It's likely that Edward finally ended his feud with the Godwine family on his death bed, and named Harold as his successor, instead of William.

King of Wales

Around 1055, Hywel Dda's great-great-grandson, Gruffydd ap Llywelyn, took his ancestor's achievements a step further. He united all the Welsh kingdoms to become the first – and possibly only – King of Wales.

60

The last of the Vikings

But, as William still believed he was the rightful King of England, Harold expected a fight for the crown. So he arranged an army along the south coast, to guard against a Norman invasion. But the first threat came from somewhere else altogether.

The King of Norway, Harald Hardrada, saw Edward's death as a chance to claim England for himself. In September 1066, he led his seaborne army up the Humber river, where he defeated English troops based in the north. Thinking that Harold's army would have a long march north, Hardrada then rested his men and waited for supplies.

But he didn't know that Harold and his men were racing north to meet them. The English troops took Hardrada completely by surprise, killing him and defeating his army at Stamford Bridge, near York.

Some accounts of the Battle of Stamford Bridge say many Vikings fled across the river. Then a huge Viking killed any English soldiers who tried to cross the bridge.

This Viking was only defeated when an English soldier floated under the bridge on a barrel, and speared him from below.

A Norman conqueror

Harold had triumphed, but he had been forced to leave the south coast unguarded. Just three days later, William of Normandy landed there with a huge army. The English forces immediately returned south, collecting more soldiers as they went. But they were too few and too exhausted to match William's army.

The two sides clashed near Hastings on October 14, 1066. Harold was killed during the battle, and William became king soon after. His victory ended the Anglo-Saxon period in England, and marked the beginning of a new chapter in the history of Britain: the rise of the Normans.

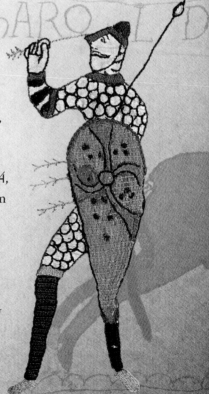

This figure from the Bayeux Tapestry is probably meant to be Harold. He's been hit in the eye with an arrow. It's unlikely he really died like this.

Index

A

abbeys, 21, 33, 36, 57, 58, 59, 60
Aelfthryth, 48, 49
Aethelbald of Mercia, 26, 28
Aethelflaed, 38, 39, 57
Alba (see also *Scotland*), 40, 41, 42, 43
Alfred the Great, 36-39, 42, 57, 59, 60
Angles, 6, 7, 9, 10, 18, 21
Anglo-Saxon Chronicle, 38, 43, 49
animals, 14-15, 27
Archbishop,
  of Canterbury, 21, 23, 29, 46
  of Lichfield, 29
  of York, 29, 52
arrows, 17, 33, 50, 61
art, 23, 54
Arthur, 8-9
Athelney, 36, 38, 41
Athelstan, King, 42-43, 57
Augustine, 20-21

B

battles, 12, 17, 25, 27, 31, 35, 36, 37, 43, 50-51, 61
  of Brunanburh, 43
  of Hastings, 61
  of Maldon, 50-51
  of Stamford Bridge, 61
Bayeux Tapestry, 60, 61
beads, 16, 19, 45
Bede, 7, 30
Beowulf, 31
Bernicia, 10, 24-25
books, 11, 22, 23, 30, 38, 56
bravery, 13, 17, 50
Britons, 6, 8-9, 10-11, 14, 16, 20, 31, 40, 43
brooches, 16, 19, 31, 45, 54
Brunanburh, Battle of, 43
Bryhtnoth of Essex, 50
burials, 18-19, 34, 40

C

Canute, King 52, 53, 54-55, 56, 57

Celtic,

  kingdoms, 10
  speakers, 10, 16, 31
  style, 11, 22, 31
ceorls, 14-15
Christianity, 5, 11, 20-23, 24, 37, 38, 44, 59
Church, the, 20-21, 23, 29, 47, 54
churches, 21, 22, 33, 42, 58, 59
clothing, 10, 16, 45
coins, 19, 29, 30, 45, 46, 59
Columba, 20
Constantine, King, 42, 43
Corfe, 48
Cornwall, 31
coronations, 46, 47
cremations, 19
crimes, 15

D

Dalriada, 10
Danelaw, 39, 41, 42, 44, 52
Deira, 10, 24-25
Denmark, 6, 32, 33, 36, 39, 45, 49, 51, 52, 53, 55, 56
dragons, 31, 34
Dublin, 41

E

Eadred, King, 43, 57
Eadric Streona, 53
Eadwig, King, 46, 57
ealdormen, 12, 50
East Angles, 10, 18
East Anglia, 33, 36, 54
Easter, 21
East Saxons, 10, 21
Edgar the Peaceful, 46-47, 48, 54, 57
Edmund Ironside, 53, 57
Edmund, King, 43, 57
Edward, King, 39, 41, 57
Edward the Confessor, 56-57, 58-59, 60
Edward the Martyr, 48-49, 57
Emma of Normandy, 51, 52, 54, 55, 56, 57

England, 28, 30, 42-43, 44,

46, 51, 52, 53, 54, 56, 57, 61
English, the, 38, 42, 54, 55, 56, 61
Essex, 21, 50
Ethelred the Unready, 48-49, 51, 52-53, 54, 56, 57

F

farmers, 12, 14, 15, 17, 39, 58
feasts, 12, 13, 24, 26, 46, 56
Five Boroughs, 39, 41
France, 19, 30, 51
food, 12, 13, 14, 15
fortified towns, 37, 59
forts, 11, 25, 36, 53

G

Germany, 6, 10, 30
Gildas, 6-7, 9
glass, 11
gods, 17, 35
Godwine, Earl, 54, 57, 60
gold, 16, 27, 29
Gruffydd ap Llwelyn, 60
Gwynedd, 10, 24, 41, 47

H

halls, 13, 14, 19
Harald Hardrada, 61
Harold Godwinson, 60-61
Harold, King, 56, 57
Harthacanute, King, 56, 57
Hastings, Battle of, 61
helmets, 19, 27, 52
heroes, 17, 31
Hild, 21, 23
houses, 10, 13, 14, 44, 45
Humber, River, 24, 39, 41, 42, 52, 61
Hywel Dda, 41, 42, 60

I

illustrations, 6, 8, 14, 23, 47, 55, 57
Iona, 20, 24, 40
Ireland, 20, 31, 33, 41
iron, 15, 19, 34
Italy, 5, 20, 30

J

Jorvik, 39, 41, 42, 43, 44-45
Jutes, 6, 7

K

Kenneth MacAlpin, 40
Kent, 10, 20, 46
kings, 8, 12-13, 15, 16, 17,
  19, 20, 24, 26, 28, 35, 40,
  47, 56, 57
knives, 15, 16, 45

L

languages, 10, 31
  Celtic, 10, 31
  English, 16, 38
  Germanic, 10, 16,
  Latin, 16, 27, 30, 38
  Old English, 16, 38
  Old Norse, 45
laws, 15, 39, 41, 58
leather, 16, 45
letters, 30, 55
libraries, 22, 33, 38
Lindisfarne, 20, 22
  Gospels, 22
London, 20, 21, 30, 37, 41,
  58-59
loyalty, 12, 13, 15, 17, 50, 55
Lundenwic, 58

M

Magnus of Norway, 56
Malcolm II, 55
Maldon, Battle of, 50-51
manuscripts, 22, 23, 42, 55
maps, 7, 10, 20, 24, 41, 50, 58
merchants, 30, 34, 35
Mercia, 10, 24, 26-29, 33, 36,
  38, 39, 41, 46, 54
metal, 11, 12, 16, 31, 33
missionaries, 20
monasteries, 20, 21, 22-23, 24,
  26, 32, 33, 38, 47, 48, 55
money, 23, 29, 51, 54, 59
monks, 7, 20, 21, 22-23, 26,
  30, 31, 33, 38, 47
monsters, 17, 31
murders, 15, 48-49, 51, 57

N

nobles, 12, 16, 23, 26, 46, 47,
  48, 52, 54, 56, 57, 60
Normandy, 50, 51, 52, 56
  Duke of, 51, 60-61
Normans, 51, 57, 61
Northumbria, 24-25, 28, 29,
  33, 35, 36, 41, 42, 43, 46, 54
Norway, 32, 33, 41, 45, 49,
  55, 56, 61

O

Offa of Mercia, 26, 28-29, 30
Offa's Dyke, 28, 29
ornaments, 10, 16, 33, 45

P

pagans, 17, 20, 35, 59
Picts, 10, 20, 24, 25, 40
poetry, 23, 31, 43, 50
Pope, 20, 21, 23
ports, 30, 58, 59
pottery, 45
prayers, 23, 33, 36
priests, 6, 12

R

rebellion, 46, 53
Rhodri Mawr, 41
Romans, 5, 10, 16, 20, 21, 29,
  44, 58-59
runes, 16, 17

S

saints, 26, 47
Saxons, 6, 7, 9, 10, 21
scholars, 8, 23, 30, 38
Scotland (see also *Alba*), 7,
  10, 31, 33, 40, 47, 55
Scots, 10, 20, 31, 40
shields, 43
ships, 6, 12, 18-19, 32, 33, 34,
  37, 44, 49
shoes, 16, 45
shops, 45
shrines, 17
silk, 35, 45
silver, 19, 24, 27, 29, 35, 59
slaves, 15, 21, 35

spears, 15, 43, 61
St. Paul's Cathedral, 58, 59
Staffordshire Hoard, 27
Stamford Bridge, Battle of, 61
stone, 22, 40, 58, 59
  carvings, 25, 44
  churches, 22, 58
  crosses, 22, 44
stories, 13, 17, 19, 31
Strathclyde, 10, 24, 40, 41, 42,
  43, 47
Sutton Hoo, 18-19, 27
Sweden, 32, 55
Swein, King, 51, 52, 53
swords, 8, 15, 27, 43

T

taxes, 51, 52, 54
thegns, 14, 15
tools, 14, 16, 19
towns, 34, 37, 44-45, 58-59
trade, 19, 30-31, 35, 45, 58, 59

V

Vikings, 32-33, 34-35, 36-37,
  38, 39, 40, 41, 42, 43, 44-45,
  49, 50-51, 52-53, 54, 59, 61
  Danish, 33, 36, 39, 41, 51,
  52-53
  Norwegian, 33, 41, 42-43, 61

W

Wales, 8-9, 20, 28, 31, 41,
  42, 60
weapons, 13, 15, 19, 27, 33, 43
Wessex, 28, 29, 32, 33, 36,
  37, 38, 39, 41, 54, 57, 60
Westminster, 58
  Abbey, 57, 58, 59, 60
West Saxons, 10, 28
Whitby, 20, 21, 23,
William of Normandy, 60-61
Winchester, 39, 41, 55
women, 15, 16, 23
wood, 13, 14, 15, 22, 34, 45,
  58, 59

Y

York, 29, 30, 39, 44-45, 61

Acknowledgements

Every effort has been made to trace and acknowledge ownership of copyright. If any rights have been omitted, the publishers offer to rectify this in any future editions following notification. The publishers are grateful to the following individuals and organizations for their permission to reproduce material on the following pages: (t=top, b=bottom, l=left, r=right, m=middle)

cover (bl) © Robert Estall photo agency/Alamy; (br) National Geographic/Getty Images; (t) © British Library Board. All Rights Reserved/The Bridgeman Art Library; (border) © British Library Board. All rights reserved, Cotton Nero D. IV, f.29 **p2-3** National Geographic/Getty Images; **p6** © The British Library Board. All Rights Reserved Add. 10292 f.164; **p8** © British Library Board. All rights reserved, Add. MS 10292 f.101; **p11 (t)** © The Trustees of the British Museum; **(b)** © Skyscan/Corbis; **p12** © The Trustees of the British Museum; **p14 (t)** © British Library Board. All Rights Reserved/The Bridgeman Art Library; **(b)** © Andrew Palmer/Alamy; **p15** © Museum of London/HIP/TopFoto; **p16** © The Trustees of the British Museum; **p17** © The Trustees of the British Museum; **p19** © The Trustees of the British Museum; **p21** © Travel and Landscape UK/Mark Sykes/Alamy; **p22** © British Library Board. All rights reserved, Cotton Nero D. IV, f.29; **p24-25 (b)** © Roger Coulam/Alamy; **p25 (t)** © David Lyons/Alamy; **p27** REUTERS/Eddie Keogh; **p28** © TopFoto; **p29 (tr)** Fitzwilliam Museum, University of Cambridge, UK/The Bridgeman Art Library **(mr)** © The Trustees of the British Museum **(br)** © The Trustees of the British Museum; **p30** © British Library Board. All rights reserved, Cotton Tiberius C. II, f.5v; **p31** © National Museums of Scotland: Licensor www.scran.ac.uk; **p33** © Museum of London, UK/The Bridgeman Art Library; **p34** Viking Ship Museum, Oslo, Norway/The Bridgeman Art Library; **p36-37** Guy Edwardes; **p38** © Ashmolean Museum, University of Oxford, UK/The Bridgeman Art Library; **p39** © Robert Estall photo agency/Alamy; **p40** © brianscotland/Alamy; **p42 (t)** © 2004 TopFoto; **p42-43** © Holmes Garden Photos/Alamy; **p44-45** © York Archaeological Trust; **p46** © The Trustees of the British Museum; **p47** © The British Library Board. All Rights Reserved, Cotton Vespasian A. VIII, f.2v; **p48** © Robert Harding Picture Library Ltd/Alamy; **p49** © Ted Spiegel/Corbis; **p52 (tl)** Universitetets Oldsamksamling, University of Oslo, Norway/Photo © AISA/The Bridgeman Art Library; **p52-53** © Ted Spiegel/Corbis; **p54** © The Trustees of the British Museum; **p55** © British Library Board. All rights reserved, Stowe 944, f.6; **p56** © British Library Board. All rights reserved, Add. 33241, f.1v; **p59** © The Trustees of the British Museum; **p60** Musée de la Tapisserie, Bayeux, France, with special authorisation of the city of Bayeux/The Bridgeman Art Library; **p61** akg-images, London/Erich Lessing/Musée de la Tapisserie

Additional illustrations by Inklink Firenze
Additional designs by Brenda Cole, Anna Gould, Stephen Moncrieff and Steve Wood
Digital design by John Russell   Picture research by Ruth King
With thanks to Barry Ager at the British Museum and Thomas Jeavons